UNFORGETTABLE

UNFORGETTABLE

IMAGES THAT CHANGED OUR LIVES

PETER DAVENPORT

CHRONICLE BOOKS
SAN FRANCISCO

Library of Congress Cataloging-in-Publication Data available.
ISBN 0-8118-3961-3

Cover design by Brett MacFadden
Manufactured in Canada

Distributed in Canada by Raincoast Books
9050 Shaughnessy Street
Vancouver, British Columbia V6P 6E5

10 9 8 7 6 5 4 3 2 1

Chronicle Books LLC
85 Second Street
San Francisco, California 94105
www.chroniclebooks.com

Note: The entries in this book are in chronological order by year,
but this is less a history in images than a history of images.
The images are presented at the occasion of their invention
or first popular appearance. Specific attribution of photographs
is given where available, and appropriate—in recent history
the same image is often multiply photographed and televised.

"Memory seems to be made up
mostly of still pictures."
— Walter Cronkite

INTRODUCTION

Humanity is defined in part by its ability to produce images, and we are forever doing so. Most images are only relevant to particular groups or activities—the vacation snapshot or the doodle on a notepad—but a few transcend their original context to become key cultural concepts, which insinuate themselves much deeper into our shared, collective memory.

This book is about these images—photographs, paintings, and cultural icons that have made such an indelible impression over the past 100 years. The *Hindenburg* disaster, the sign in the Hollywood Hills, late-night diners at the counter in Edward Hopper's *Nighthawks,* the swastika, the smiley face: we know them all. They come to the mind's eye with just a mention or, in the case of this book, a caption.

What is it that makes these images stick in the mind, while others quickly fade? For the most part, images become unforgettable because they define moments and movements that are a part of our common culture. They have become part of a visual vocabulary in a world where we increasingly communicate by using pictures rather than words.

Imagine a dictionary of visual literacy, where there are no words, just pictures to represent our common experiences: joy, sorrow, love, hate, humor, surprise, and wonder. For such communication to work, the images—like the images in this book—must be common currency, their significance felt as much as understood.

Some of these images are strong emotional triggers. Frames from the Zapruder film of the Kennedy assassination instantly remind us where we were and how we felt at that moment of history, as now do images from September 11. These, like the images of the first lunar landing, are instantly fixed in our memories. Others, like John Travolta in disco regalia, may be less momentous but also surprisingly stay in our minds. What they all have in common is that we all have them in common.

What we remember is part of our consciousness. So it is with society—what it remembers collectively determines its view of itself, its identity. And memory is mostly pictures.

WRIGHT BROTHERS' FIRST TAKEOFF
John T. Daniels

1903

FINGERPRINT
First used in a criminal conviction

1903

SHOOTING THE AUDIENCE
The Great Train Robbery
Directed by Edwin S. Porter

1903

LES DEMOISELLES D'AVIGNON
Pablo Picasso

1907

MODEL-T FORD
First production model
Designed by Henry Ford

1908

THE *TITANIC* SINKS
Artist's rendition

1912

NUDE DESCENDING A STAIRCASE NO.2
Marcel Duchamp

1912

OLYMPIC GAMES SYMBOL
Designed by Baron Pierre de Coubertin

1913

CHARLIE CHAPLIN
The Tramp
Directed by Charlie Chaplin

1915

COCA-COLA BOTTLE
Designed by Alex Samuelson

1916

FOUNTAIN

Marcel Duchamp

1917

UNCLE SAM RECRUITING POSTER
J. M. Flagg

1917

NO MAN'S LAND
Photographer unknown

1917

WHITE ON WHITE
Kasimir Malevich

1919

LENIN ADDRESSING TROOPS IN MOSCOW
G. P. Goldshtein

1920

SWASTIKA

Adopted by Hilter as symbol of the Nazi party

1920

INKBLOT TEST
Developed by Hermann Rorschach

1921

CHANEL PERFUME BOTTLE
Designed by Coco Chanel

1921

HAMMER AND SICKLE
Adopted as the symbol of the U.S.S.R.

1922

MUMMY CASE OF TUTANKHAMUN
Discovered by Howard Carter

1922

LE VIOLON D'INGRES
Man Ray

1924

HOLLYWOOD SIGN
Hollywoodland Real Estate Group

1924

SCREAMING NURSE
Battleship Potemkin
Directed by Sergei Eisenstein

1925

JOSEPHINE BAKER IN SKIRT OF BANANAS
Roger-Viollet

1926

AL JOLSON
The Jazz Singer
Directed by Alan Crosland

1927

CHARLES LINDBERGH AND THE *SPIRIT OF ST. LOUIS*, PARIS
Photographer unknown

1927

FUTURISTIC CITY
Metropolis
Directed by Fritz Lang

1927

ELECTROCUTION OF RUTH SNYDER
Tom Howard

1928

SLICING THE EYEBALL
Un Chein Andalou
Directed by Luis Buñuel/Salvador Dalí

1928

MICKEY MOUSE
Created by Walt Disney

1928

AL CAPONE
Photographer unknown

1929

COMPOSITION WITH RED, BLUE, YELLOW, AND BLACK
Piet Mondrian

1929

BETTY BOOP
Created by Grim Natwick

1930

AMERICAN GOTHIC
Grant Wood

1930

GRETA GARBO
Clarence Sinclair Bull

BORIS KARLOFF
Frankenstein
Directed by James Whale

1931

THE PERSISTENCE OF MEMORY (SOFT WATCHES)
Salvador Dalí

1931

LUNCHTIME ATOP A SKYSCRAPER

1932

KING KONG
King Kong
Directed by Merian C. Cooper/Ernest Schoedsack

1933

LOCH NESS MONSTER
Robert Wilson

1934

MONOPOLY GAME BOARD
Created by Charles B. Darrow/Parker Brothers

1934

THE TREASON OF IMAGES (THIS IS NOT A PIPE)
René Magritte

1935

FRED ASTAIRE AND GINGER ROGERS
Top Hat
Directed by Mark Sandrich

1935

NUREMBERG RALLY
Triumph of the Will
Directed by Leni Reifenstahl

1935

JESSE OWENS SALUTING, BERLIN OLYMPICS
Anthony Camerano

1936

MILK DROP CORONET
Harold E. Edgerton

1936

FIRST *LIFE* MAGAZINE COVER
Fort Peck Dam
Photograph by Margaret Bourke-White

1936

MIGRANT MOTHER
Dorothea Lange

1936

BREAKFAST IN FUR
Cup, saucer, spoon
Meret Oppenheim

1936

DEATH OF A LOYALIST SOLDIER
Robert Capa

1936

FALLING WATER
Architect Frank Lloyd Wright

1937

SNOW WHITE
Snow White and the Seven Dwarfs
Produced by Walt Disney

1937

GUERNICA
Pablo Picasso

1937

THE *HINDENBURG* DISASTER
Sam Shere

1937

SUPERMAN
Created by Jerry Siegel/Joe Shuster

1938

RECLINING FIGURE
Henry Moore

1938

COWARDLY LION, DOROTHY, TIN MAN, SCARECROW
The Wizard of Oz
Directed by Victor Fleming

1939

CONEY ISLAND
Weegee

1940

CHARLIE CHAPLIN
The Great Dictator
Directed by Charlie Chaplin

1940

KANE CAMPAIGNING
Citizen Kane
Directed by Orson Welles

1941

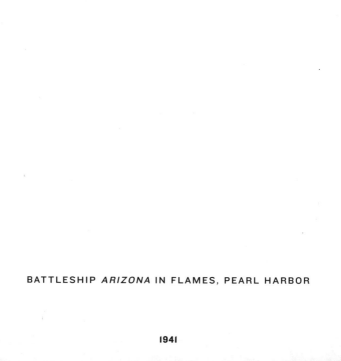

BATTLESHIP *ARIZONA* IN FLAMES, PEARL HARBOR

1941

FRANKLIN D. ROOSEVELT ADDRESSING THE NATION

1941

MOUNT RUSHMORE
Sculptor Gutzon Borglum

1941

BETTY GRABLE
Pinup

1942

NIGHTHAWKS
Edward Hopper

1942

ROSIE THE RIVETER
J. Howard Miller

1943

D-DAY, OMAHA BEACH
Robert Capa

1944

RAISING THE FLAG ON IWO JIMA
Joe Rosenthal

1945

RAISING THE SOVIET FLAG OVER THE REICHSTAG
Yevgeny Khaldei

1945

ANNE FRANK
Self-portrait

1945

BOMBER CREW IN FRONT OF THE *ENOLA GAY*
Photographer unknown

1945

NAGASAKI AFTER THE BOMB
Aerial view
George Silk

1945

SAILOR KISSING A GIRL ON VJ-DAY, TIMES SQUARE
Alfred Eisenstaedt

1945

DOUGLAS MACARTHUR WADES ASHORE
Carl Mydans

1945

ATOMIC TEST ON BIKINI ATOLL
Automatic camera recording

1946

Designed by Louis Reard

1946

MAHATMA GANDHI
Margaret Bourke-White

1946

AK-47
Designed by Mikhail Kalashnikov

1947

BABE RUTH BOWS OUT
Nat Fein

1948

DEWEY DEFEATS TRUMAN
Byron Rollins

1948

CHAIRMAN MAO
Official portrait

1949

CHARLIE BROWN
Created by Charles M. Schulz

1950

AUTUMN RHYTHM

Jackson Pollock

1950

UFO
Photographer unknown

1950

THE KISS IN THE STREET BY THE HÔTEL DE VILLE, PARIS
Robert Doisneau

1950

ELIZABETH TAYLOR AND MONTGOMERY CLIFT KISSING
A Place in the Sun
Directed by George Stevens

1951

MODEL OF DNA STRAND
Discovered by Francis Crick/James Watson

1953

PORTRAIT OF ELIZABETH II ON HER CORONATION
Cecil Beaton

1953

SCREAMING POPE (HEAD VI)
Francis Bacon

1953

BURT LANCASTER AND DEBORAH KERR
From Here to Eternity
Fred Zinnemann

1953

PLAYBOY BUNNY LOGO
Designed by Art Paul

1953

FENDER STRATOCASTER GUITAR
Designed by Leo Fender

1954

GREYHOUND BUS
Designed by Raymond Loewy

1954

MARLON BRANDO
The Wild One
Directed by Laslo Benedek

1954

SLEEPING BEAUTY'S CASTLE, DISNEYLAND
Designed by Herbert Ryman

1955

CHAPEL OF NOTRE DAME, RONCHAMP
Architect Le Corbusier

1955

JAMES DEAN ON TIMES SQUARE
Dennis Stock

1955

MARILYN MONROE STANDING OVER SUBWAY GRATING
The Seven Year Itch
Directed by Billy Wilder

1955

DAVY CROCKETT HAT

1955

ELVIS PRESLEY SINGING "HOUND DOG"
Charles Trainor

1956

ROBBY THE ROBOT
Forbidden Planet
Directed by Fred M. Wilcox

1956

SPUTNIK

Designed by Sergei Korolev

1957

CHESS MATCH
The Seventh Seal
Directed by Ingmar Bergman

1957

COMPUTER CIRCUIT BOARD

1958

THREE FLAGS
Jasper Johns

1958

PEACE SYMBOL
Symbol for the Campaign for Nuclear Disarmament
Designed by Gerald Holtom

1958

BARBIE DOLL
Created by Ruth Handler

1959

CADILLAC ELDORADO CONVERTIBLE
Designed by Clarence Johnson

1959

CROP-DUSTER CHASE

North by Northwest

Directed by Alfred Hitchcock

1959

CHARIOT RACE
Ben Hur
Directed by William Wyler

1959

FIDEL CASTRO ADDRESSES THE PEOPLE
AFTER ENTERING HAVANA
Bob Henriques

1959

NIKITA KRUSCHEV AND RICHARD NIXON
(KITCHEN DEBATE)
Elliott Erwitt

1959

GUGGENHEIM MUSEUM, NEW YORK
Architect Frank Lloyd Wright

1959

ASCENDING AND DESCENDING

M. C. Escher

1960

ANITA EKBERG IN THE TREVI FOUNTAIN
La Dolce Vita
Directed by Federico Fellini

1960

SHOWER SCREAM

Psycho

Directed by Alfred Hitchcock

1960

MCDONALD'S GOLDEN ARCHES LOGO
Created by Jim Schindler

1962

CAMPBELL'S SOUP CAN
Andy Warhol

1962

JAMES BOND OPENING TITLES
Gun's-eye view
Designed by Maurice Binder

1962

CUBAN MISSILE BASE
U.S. reconnaissance photograph

1962

MINISKIRT
Designed by Mary Quant

1963

SELF-IMMOLATION OF QUANG DUC, SAIGON
Malcolm Browne

1963

WHAAM!
Roy Lichtenstein

1963

LYNDON JOHNSON SWORN IN ON *AIR FORCE ONE*
Cecil Stoughton

1963

THE MURDER OF LEE HARVEY OSWALD
Robert Jackson

1963

JOHN F. KENNEDY JR. SALUTES HIS FATHER'S COFFIN
Harry Leder

1963

THE MAN WITH NO NAME
A Fistful of Dollars
Directed by Sergio Leone

1964

SHOOTING THE APPLE
Harold E. Edgerton

1964

THE BEATLES FIRST ARRIVE IN NEW YORK AT JFK AIRPORT
Bill Eppridge

1964

MALCOLM X MEETS MARTIN LUTHER KING JR.

1964

MUHAMMAD ALI KNOCKS OUT SONNY LISTON
Neil Leifer

1965

JULIE ANDREWS
The Sound of Music
Directed by Robert Wise

1965

LOVE
Robert Indiana

1966

MR. SPOCK GIVING THE VULCAN PEACE SIGN
Star Trek
Created by Gene Roddenberry

1966

SGT. PEPPER'S LONELY HEARTS CLUB BAND
The Beatles
Designed by Peter Blake/Jane Haworth

1967

BOY PLACING FLOWER IN RIFLE BARREL
Bernie Boston

1967

CHE GUEVARA POSTER
Photograph by Alberto Korda

1967

JIMI HENDRIX BURNING HIS GUITAR
Monterey Pop Festival
Ed Caraeff

1967

STREET EXECUTION OF A VIETCONG PRISONER
Eddie Adams

1968

ASSASSINATION OF MARTIN LUTHER KING JR.
Joseph Louw

1968

ROBERT F. KENNEDY SHOT
Bill Eppridge

1968

BLACK POWER SALUTE
Mexico City Olympics

1968

EARTHRISE FROM THE MOON
William Anders, *Apollo 8*

1968

BUZZ ALDRIN ON THE MOON
Neil Armstrong

1969

PETER FONDA AND DENNIS HOPPER
Easy Rider
Directed by Dennis Hopper

1969

CHARLES MANSON
Life magazine cover

1969

JOHN AND YOKO'S BED-IN FOR WORLD PEACE

1969

CANNABIS LEAF

1971

SMILEY FACE BUTTON
Designed by Harvey R. Ball

1971

CHILDREN FLEEING AN AMERICAN NAPALM STRIKE
Huynh Cong Ut

1972

TERRORIST ON THE BALCONY
Munich Olympics

1972

MANHATTAN ON COMPLETION OF THE WORLD TRADE CENTER
View from the Staten Island Ferry

1973

SYDNEY OPERA HOUSE
Architect Jørn Utzon

1973

DARK SIDE OF THE MOON
Pink Floyd
Designed by Hipgnosis

1973

BARCODE
Invented by George J. Laurer

1973

NIXON WAVING FROM HELICOPTER STEPS
Oliver F. Atkins

1974

EVACUATION OF THE U.S. EMBASSY, SAIGON
Hubert Van Es

1975

I LOVE NEW YORK
Milton Glaser

1975

VIEW OF THE WORLD FROM 9TH AVENUE
New Yorker magazine cover
Saul Steinberg

1976

MISS PIGGY
The Muppet Show
Created by Jim Henson

1976

DARTH VADER
Star Wars
Directed by George Lucas

1977

JOHN TRAVOLTA
Saturday Night Fever
Directed by John Badham

1977

FARAH FAWCETT
Poster

1977

POMPIDOU CENTRE, PARIS
Architects Piano/Rogers

1977

MOTHERSHIP LANDING
Close Encounters of the Third Kind
Directed by Steven Spielberg

1977

THE VILLAGE PEOPLE PERFORMING "Y.M.C.A."

1978

PAC MAN
Designed by Toru Iwatani
Bally/Midway/Namco

1980

SPACE SHUTTLE LAUNCH
NASA

1981

FLYING BICYCLE
E.T. the Extra-Terrestrial
Directed by Steven Spielberg

1982

RAMBO
First Blood
Directed by Ted Kotcheff

1982

VIETNAM VETERANS' MEMORIAL, WASHINGTON, D.C.
Designed by Maya Lin

1982

FIRST UNTETHERED SPACEWALK
Astronaut Bruce McCandless
NASA

1984

THE SPACE SHUTTLE *CHALLENGER* EXPLODES

1986

GOLD MINE, BRAZIL
Sebastião Salgado

1986

MICHAEL JACKSON AND BUBBLES
Jeff Koons

1988

SPERM MEETS EGG
Lennart Nilsson

1988

BIRD COVERED IN OIL
Exxon Valdez disaster

1989

MAN CONFRONTING TANKS, BEIJING
Stuart Franklin

1989

SMASHING THE BERLIN WALL
Anthony Suau

1989

THE SIMPSONS (ON THE SOFA)
The Simpsons
Created by Matt Groening

1989

NELSON MANDELA UPON HIS RELEASE FROM PRISON

1990

MADONNA IN JEAN-PAUL GAULTIER CORSET
Blonde Ambition tour

1990

DEMI MOORE PREGNANT
Cover of *Vanity Fair* magazine
Photograph by Annie Leibovitz

1991

CRUISE MISSILE
Baghdad

1991

BLAZING OIL FIELDS
Kuwait

1991

AIDS RIBBON
Designed by the Visual AIDS Artist Caucus

1991

THE PHYSICAL IMPOSSIBILITY OF DEATH IN THE MIND OF
SOMEONE LIVING (SHARK)
Damien Hirst

1991

RODNEY KING BEATING
George Holliday

1991

BARNEY THE DINOSAUR
Barney & Friends
Created by Sheryl Leach

1992

BUZZ LIGHTYEAR AND WOODY
Toy Story
Directed by John Lasseter

1995

CHILD VICTIM CRADLED BY FIREMAN
Oklahoma City bombing
Charles Porter IV

1995

OJ SIMPSON TRIES ON MURDER GLOVE

1995

PILLARS OF MATTER IN THE EAGLE NEBULA
Hubble Telescope
Jeff Hester/Paul Scowen/NASA

1995

UNABOMBER SUSPECT
Police sketch

1996

BILL CLINTON AND MONICA LEWINSKY EMBRACE AT
A FUND RAISING EVENT
Dirk Halstead

1996

VIEW OF MARS SURFACE FROM PATHFINDER
NASA

1997

DOLLY THE SHEEP
Cloned by Ian Wilmut

1997

KATE WINSLET AND LEONARDO DI CAPRIO
Titanic
Directed by James Cameron

1997

SEA OF FLOWERS AT KENSINGTON GARDENS
Death of Princess Diana

1997

HARRY POTTER AND THE SORCERER'S STONE
Harry riding a broom
By J. K. Rowling/Illustration by Mary GrandPré

1998